About This Book

Title: *Fish*

Step: 3

Word Count: 170

Skills in Focus: Consonant digraphs

Tricky Words: water, ocean, breathe, eat, away, hide, live, other, salt, sank

Ideas for Using This Book

Before Reading:

- **Comprehension:** Look at the title and cover image together. Ask readers what they know about fish. What new things do they think they might learn in this book?
- **Accuracy:** Practice saying the tricky words listed on page 1.
- **Phonics and Phonemic Awareness:** Have students look at the book's title. Help them blend the sounds they see in the word *fish*. Bring attention to the *sh* in the word. Explain that this is a digraph, two letters that make one sound when they are together. Ask readers to say the word in the title again and help them tap out the sounds in the word. Emphasize the /sh/ sound and say it louder as you tap. Ask readers to watch and listen for other examples of *ch*, *th*, *sh*, and *ng* in the text.

During Reading:

- Have readers point under each word as they read it.
- **Decoding:** If readers are stuck on a word, help them say each sound and blend the sounds together smoothly. Be sure to point out any words with digraphs.
- **Comprehension:** Invite students to talk about what new things they are learning about fish while reading. What are they learning that they didn't know before?

After Reading:

Discuss the book. Some ideas for questions:

- Where are some places that fish live?
- Have you ever been to an aquarium? What kinds of fish did you see there?

Fish

Text by Haley Williams

Reading Consultant
Deborah MacPhee, PhD
Professor, School of Teaching and Learning
Illinois State University

PICTURE WINDOW BOOKS
a capstone imprint

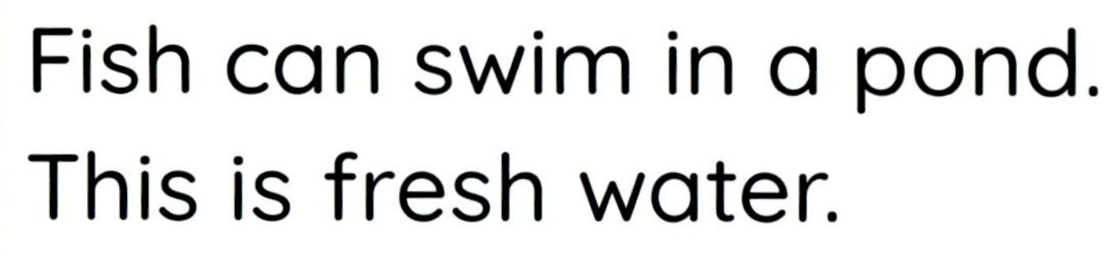

Fish can swim in a pond.
This is fresh water.

Fish can swim in the ocean.
This is salt water.

Fish do not
have lungs.
Gills help fish
breathe in water.

Fish have fins. Fins help them swim.

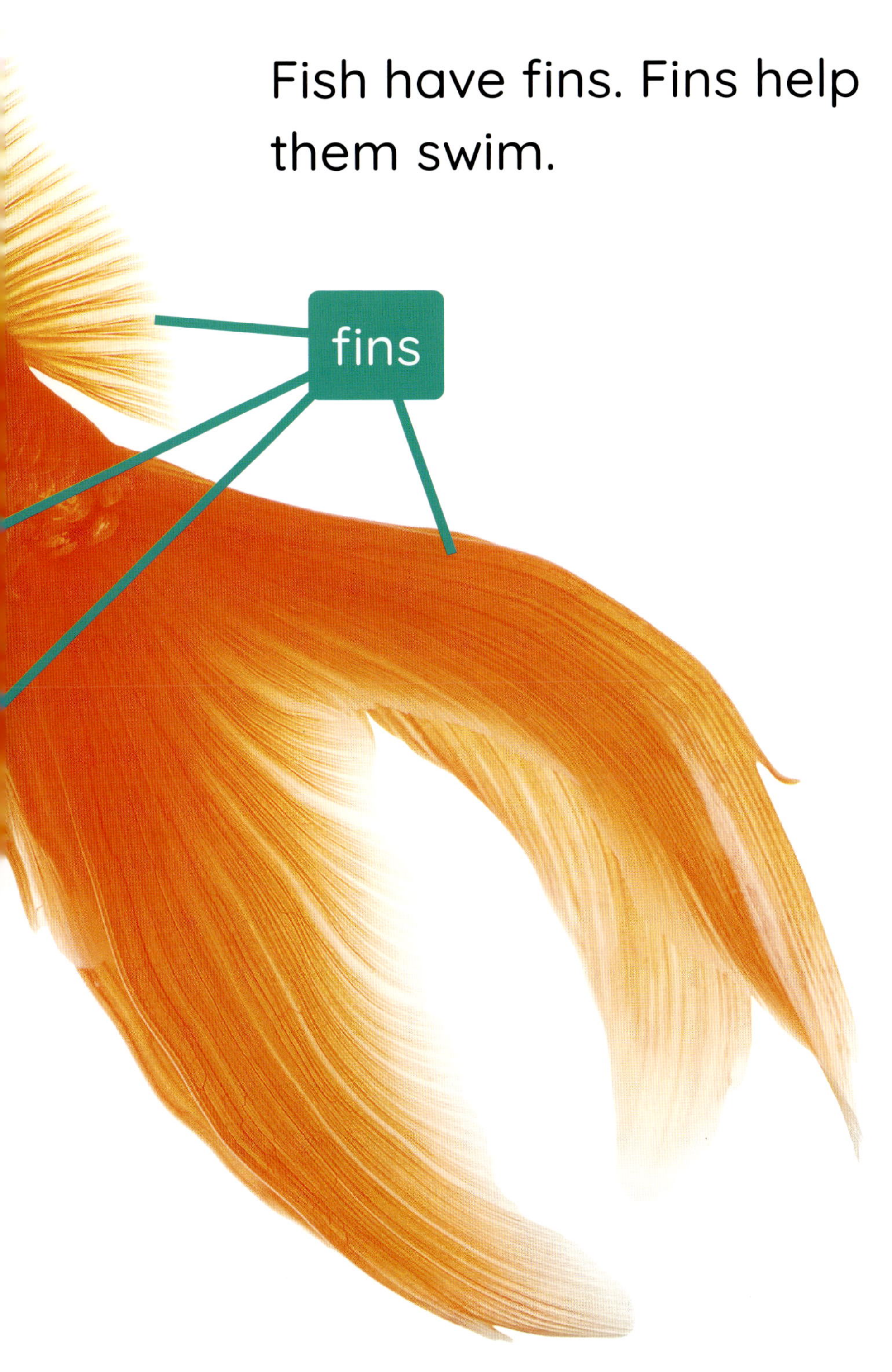

This fish has black spots.

This fish puffs up when it is mad.

Fish can be big.
Sharks are big fish.

Some fish are not big.
They may swim in schools.

Fish eat many things.
They eat kelp.

They eat bugs,
crabs, and other fish.

Small fish swim
away from big fish.

They find spots to hide in the rocks and in shells.

A shark jumps from the water. It makes a big splash. It chomps down on a snack. Munch! Crunch!

This ship sank to
the ocean floor.

The ship sits in the sand.
Fish swim in the wreck.

Kids can watch fish swim in a tank.

The tank has lots of rocks for fish to live in.

A bunch of fish swim in the tank. Which one do you like?

More Ideas:

Phonemic Awareness Activity

Practicing Digraphs:

Write the story words *fish*, *this*, and *rock*. Have readers tap out the sounds down their left arms, starting by their shoulders and moving toward their wrists. Ask readers how many sounds they hear in the word. Remind them that the *s* and *h* make one sound when they are together, even though they are two different letters. So do the *t* and *h*. The *c* and *k* make one sound when they are together too. Continue with other *sh*, *th*, and *ck* words, such as *ship*, *splash*, *them*, *wreck*, and *black*.

Extended Learning Activity

Fish Habitat:

Ask readers to think about where a fish might live and what it might eat. Have them draw a picture of a fish in its habitat. Then ask readers to share three sentences about the fish and its habitat. Challenge students to include words with different digraphs in their sentences.

Published by Picture Window Books, an imprint of Capstone
1710 Roe Crest Drive, North Mankato, Minnesota 56003
capstonepub.com

Library of Congress Cataloging-in-Publication Data is available on the Library of Congress website.

ISBN: 9798875277467 (hardback)
ISBN: 9798875277429 (paperback)
ISBN: 9798875277405 (eBook PDF)

Image Credits: Getty: atese, 14–15, 24, CarlFourie, 20–21, LFPuntel, 19, Ute Niemann, 1, 8; Shutterstock: Brandon B, 12, Derek Heasley, 10, DJ Mattaar, front cover, Dobermaraner, 11, Jung Hsuan, 9, Katerina Maksymenko, 2–3, Kletr, 4, leungchopan, 22–23, mcmortgreen, 13, mc_pongsatorn, 5, Nejat Semerci, 18, Sergey Uryadnikov, 16–17, Vangert, 6–7, back cover

Printed and bound in China. PO 6460